Library and Archives Canada Cataloguing in Publication

Smith, Leonard B., 1945-
My smile / Leonard B. Smith. -- Rev. ed.

ISBN 978-0-9685748-2-9

1. Teeth--Care and hygiene--Juvenile literature.
2. Teeth--Juvenile literature. I. Title.

RK63.S53 2012 j617.6'01 C2012-904157-2

MY Smile

"My smile begins before I'm born!"

Proper nutrition for mom is essential so baby's teeth develop as they should before birth.

"I may not be able to tell you if I have a toothache."

When baby's first teeth appear, so does the threat of tooth decay and gum disease. As a parent, there's so much you can do to protect your child's oral health and avoid problems.

"You should supervise my brushing and flossing 'til I'm 8 or 9."

The *MY Smile* book is full of important tips on kids' oral health care, all sharing a common theme that "Prevention is the BEST treatment" to ensure young smiles last a lifetime.

"Hey Mom! Hey Dad! Did you know..."

Special Needs Page 29 - 30

"My special needs mean I need regular dental care."

Dental neglect of children with special medical conditions or disabilities can lead to serious, even life-threatening medical complications, not to mention problems with self-esteem and social acceptance later on in life.

Important Facts Page 31 - 36

"What you don't know about snack foods can hurt me."

Some snack foods keep teeth healthy. Others cause dental problems. Saliva is important to dental health. Plaque leads to decay. Learn more about these important facts.

My Dental Diary Page 37 - 38

"You should keep a record of when my permanent teeth start to appear."

Use the Dental Diary included at the back of this book to record when your child's permanent teeth emerge. Besides being a lasting keepsake, this record will help you, your child and your child's dentist keep track of dental development.

Prevention is the BEST treatment®

“Before I’m born...”

"My baby teeth won't all be in place until I'm about 3 years old."

"My permanent teeth begin developing at or after birth."

By the time the primary dentition (baby teeth) are all visible, the permanent teeth are developing.

Permanent teeth lay hidden under the gums, occupying most of the upper and lower jaw area. Once the crown of a tooth is in the mouth, it does not grow larger.

Did You Know?

"My teeth start to form 7 weeks after you become pregnant."

Baby teeth are almost fully developed beneath the gums at birth.

- Incisors (front teeth) begin to develop at 7 weeks into pregnancy and calcify (harden with enamel) at about 15 weeks.
- The First Molars begin to develop at 8 weeks and calcify at about 16 weeks.
- The Cuspids (eye teeth) begin to develop at 7 1/2 weeks and calcify at about 17 weeks.
- The Second Molars begin to develop at 10 weeks and calcify at about 19 weeks.

Of growing importance.

Did You Know?

"I could be born too early if you have gum disease."

Every year in the United States, periodontal infection (gum disease) in mothers is believed to cause up to 18 per cent of the 250,000 premature babies born weighing less than 5.5 pounds.

"It's important for my Mom and Dad to have healthy teeth and gums that are free of dental bacteria."

"When you eat, you're feeding me too."

Ideal prenatal nutrition promotes the development of a healthy baby.

That includes the formation of healthy teeth and soft tissues of the mouth.

"I need important NUTRIENTS to ensure that I have healthy teeth, gums and more!"

The growth and development of your child's future teeth and oral soft tissues can be compromised by deficiencies in:

- Vitamin A
- Vitamin B1 (Thiamine)
- Vitamin B2 (Niacin)
- Vitamin B6 (Pyridoxine)
- Vitamin B12 (Cobalamin)
- Vitamin C (Ascorbic Acid)
- Vitamin D
- Vitamin E (Tocopherol)
- Vitamin K
- Calcium
- Folic Acid
- Iodine
- Iron
- Magnesium
- Phosphorous
- Selenium
- Zinc

Check with your physician or a qualified nutritionist to ensure that your diet is balanced and includes these important nutrients.

The right stuff...

"Mom, you need to eat the right stuff before I'm born so I have the best chance to develop as I should."

Vitamin A

Essential to development of vision and growth of skeleton, skin and tissue. Helps prevent cell damage.
Found in: *deep yellow and orange vegetables and fruits, green leafy vegetables, fish-liver oils, egg yolks, milk, butter.*

Vitamin B1 (Thiamine)

Assists in carbohydrate metabolism.
Found in: *liver, meat, cereal, milk, nuts, legumes (beans, peas, lentils, peanuts, soybeans).*

Vitamin B2 (Riboflavin)

Essential for metabolism.
Found in: *cheese, yogurt, enriched grain breads, fish, milk, liver, eggs, green leafy vegetables.*

Vitamin B3 (Niacin)

Promotes normal digestion, supports functioning of nervous system, assists energy metabolism.
Found in: *green leafy vegetables, nuts, poultry, fish.*

Vitamin B6 (Pyridoxine)

Aids in red blood cell production, immune development, carbohydrate metabolism.
Found in: *lean meat, liver, seeds, milk, whole grains, egg yolks.*

Vitamin B12 (Cobalamin)

Helps produce red blood cells, assists metabolism.
Found in: *lean meat, kidney, liver, eggs, poultry, fish, shellfish.*

Vitamin C (Ascorbic Acid)

Promotes resistance to infection, helps prevent and repair damage to tissues.
Found in: *citrus fruits, peppers, cabbage, berries, potatoes, tomatoes.*

Vitamin D

Helps body absorb calcium, regulates use of calcium and phosphorous in bone formation.
Found in: *fortified milk, butter, fish-liver oils, egg yolks, sunlight.*

Vitamin E (Tocopherol)

Biologic antioxidant protects cells during development.
Found in: *peanut and corn oils, wheat germ, green leafy vegetables.*

Vitamin K

Assists development of blood-clotting protein, inhibits loss of calcium.
Found in: *liver, green leafy vegetables such as spinach.*

Calcium

Helps build teeth and bones, promotes muscle and nerve functions.
Found in: *dairy products, canned salmon, broccoli, tofu, soy drinks.*

Folic Acid

Essential to reduce risk of serious central nervous system defects in fetal development during early pregnancy.
Found in: *orange juice, liver, kidney, green leafy vegetables, legumes, cheese.*

Iodine

Aids in development of thyroid hormones which control metabolism.
Found in: *iodized salt, seafood.*

Iron

Promotes production of red blood cells and prevents anemia.
Found in: *liver, meat, shellfish, legumes.*

Magnesium

Assists in bone formation, muscle development.
Found in: *green leafy vegetables, whole grains, legumes, cocoa.*

Phosphorous

Helps build bones and teeth.
Found in: *liver, kidney, legumes.*

Selenium

Antioxidant which helps protect cells during development.
Found in: *fish, shellfish, meat, eggs, grains, vegetables.*

Zinc

Helps develop taste perception, aids in bone formation, enhances healing.
Found in: *fish, meat, grains, cheese, nuts.*

"I have 20 baby teeth forming."

Primary (Baby) Teeth

Upper Teeth

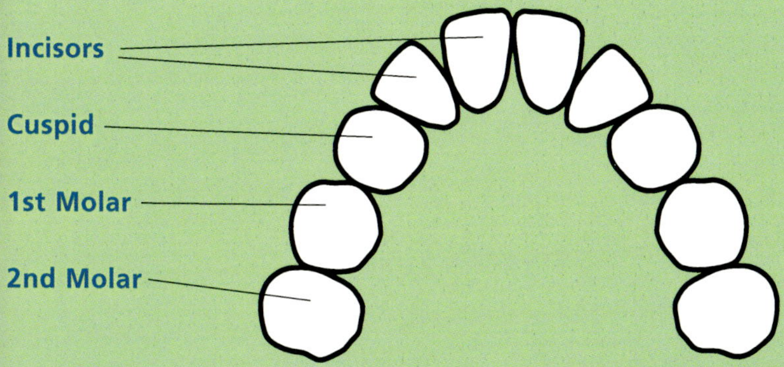

Lower Teeth

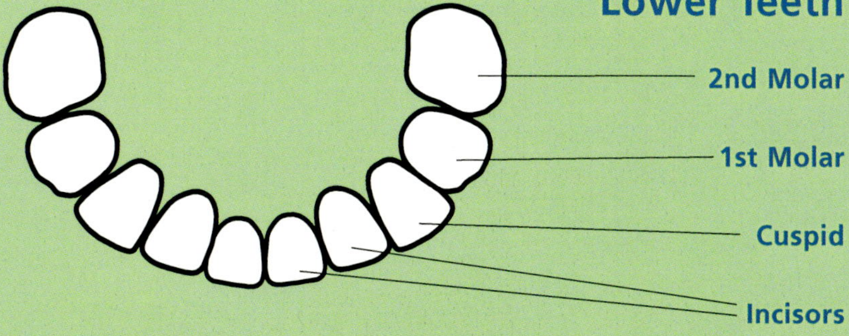

There are four types of primary teeth:

- 8 Incisors used for cutting food
- 4 Cuspids used for gripping and tearing food
- 4 First Molars used for chewing and grinding food
- 4 Second Molars used for chewing and grinding food

"My baby teeth are important. They have to last a long time."

Primary (baby) teeth play a significant role in your child's development.

- They allow your child to bite and chew the food needed for healthy growth and development.
- They help hold the lips in the right position to develop a pleasant smile.
- They provide necessary tools for speech development and act as a guide to the position of the permanent teeth.
- The last baby teeth usually fall out of your child's mouth by about age 13.

Did You Know?

Unhealthy baby teeth can result in unhealthy permanent teeth.

"Breast feeding offers
me the best source
of nutrients."

"As soon as my first teeth appear, decay can begin."

Dental plaque - the cells, food and bacteria which cause dental decay - can be found shortly after the first teeth appear in the mouth. Its presence can increase as more teeth erupt.

If this plaque is not removed from the teeth daily, cavities can begin to develop.

If you see any spots or discoloration on your child's teeth, take your child to a dentist immediately. Do not wait!

No child is too young for a visit to the dentist.

Did You Know?

"Decay prevention must begin immediately after my first feeding."

Use a moist washcloth to clean your baby's gum pads of milk residue after every feeding.

"You can protect my teeth
from bottle decay."

"If I'm allowed to feed all night, my teeth could become decayed."

- The bacteria responsible for decay (streptococcus mutans) change sugars into acid, causing tooth decay.
- Soft drinks, fruit juices, milk, sweetened water and honey contain sugars which are food for decay-causing bacteria.
- Unrestricted feeding habits and repeated exposure to sugars over extended periods of time during the day or night influence the extent of decay.
- Because of the need for regular cleaning, continuous or frequent feedings of any kind can be hazardous.
- Remember to remove the plaque from the gums and all tooth surfaces after any kind of feeding. Use a clean washcloth, a soft brush and/or floss.

"Please don't dip my pacifier into sugar, jam or honey."

Did You Know?

Top front teeth usually decay first.

- Bottle-fed milk or juice at bed time can contribute to infant tooth decay.
- Top front baby teeth usually decay first because they don't get enough saliva – a natural defense against decay – from the salivary glands in the lower part of the mouth, under the tongue, and in the cheeks at the back of the mouth.

"My baby teeth need your
tender loving care."

Decay is a disease...and dangerous!

- Decay is an infectious disease.
- Decay continues to infect more of the tooth and can rapidly infect other teeth.
- A decay-infected tooth may develop an abscess: as soon as the nerve becomes infected, it dies and the cells degenerate into pus.
- An abscess can mean that your child could be swallowing a cup of pus a day!

Decayed baby teeth must be repaired!

Did You Know?

"You can transmit cavity-producing bacteria to me with a kiss."

While babies need to be hugged and kissed, kisses also transfer cavity-producing oral bacteria from parents. That's why it's so important for parents to have good oral health and to pay special attention to their baby's teeth.

Over 25 years of studies have shown that the natural sweetener "xylitol", available as a sugar substitute in a growing number of chewing gums, snack foods and beverages, has proven effective in reducing oral bacteria.

"I may not be able
to tell you..."

"How would you know if I have a toothache... or something worse?"

- Your child may have a toothache but may not be able to tell you.
- An unhappy disposition, poor sleep patterns and feeding habits are signs that your child may have a toothache.
- Children may suffer from a toothache for so long that they may think the pain is "normal".
- Look into your child's mouth. If the top front teeth are broken, discolored or spotted, your little one may be suffering.

Did You Know?

"The shape of my jaw and the position of my teeth can be changed by soothers, thumbs and fingers."

"I can begin to have my bite corrected when I'm as young as three."

"My teeth need space to grow."

Did You Know?

"My first dental visit should be before my first birthday."

"Spaces between my teeth are important."

- Good spacing of baby teeth is a positive sign that there will be adequate room for permanent teeth to replace the baby teeth.
- Little or no spacing between the baby teeth is an indication that dental crowding will be a problem in the future.

"My dentist will examine my neck, jaw, all over the inside of my mouth, my gums and teeth."

Dentists look at more than just teeth. They should:

- Inspect the throat, roof of the mouth, cheeks, tongue, lymph glands, floor of the mouth, lips and gums.
- Assess your child's bite relationship by taking a complete look at how the jaw is positioned - front to back, up and down, side to side.
- Look at how much space there is in the jaw for the permanent teeth to come in.

After all this is complete, the teeth are checked for cavities.

"You can help me avoid
dental mishaps."

"Mouth injuries often occur when I start to stand up, walk and play!"

Injuries to the mouth and teeth of children are preventable. You want to do ALL you can to avoid these injuries. ***Prevention is the BEST treatment.®***

- **Children should not be put into walkers.**
- **All stairs should be blocked or gated to prevent children from falling.**
- **Dental trauma and injuries occur most often on stairs, in bathtubs and from sharp edges on furniture and fireplaces.**
- **Anywhere playground equipment (swings, teeter totters), baseball bats or golf clubs are being used, be especially cautious to keep the toddlers away to avoid serious injury.**
- **Children can bite through electrical cords causing severe burns to the mouth and possible electrocution.**

"Smiling is all about feeling good about myself."

Did You Know?

"My permanent teeth should start appearing by age 6. Except for my wisdom teeth, they should all be in my mouth by the time I'm 13."

"From age 6 to 13, I lose my baby teeth, get my permanent teeth and meet new friends at school."

Permanent Teeth

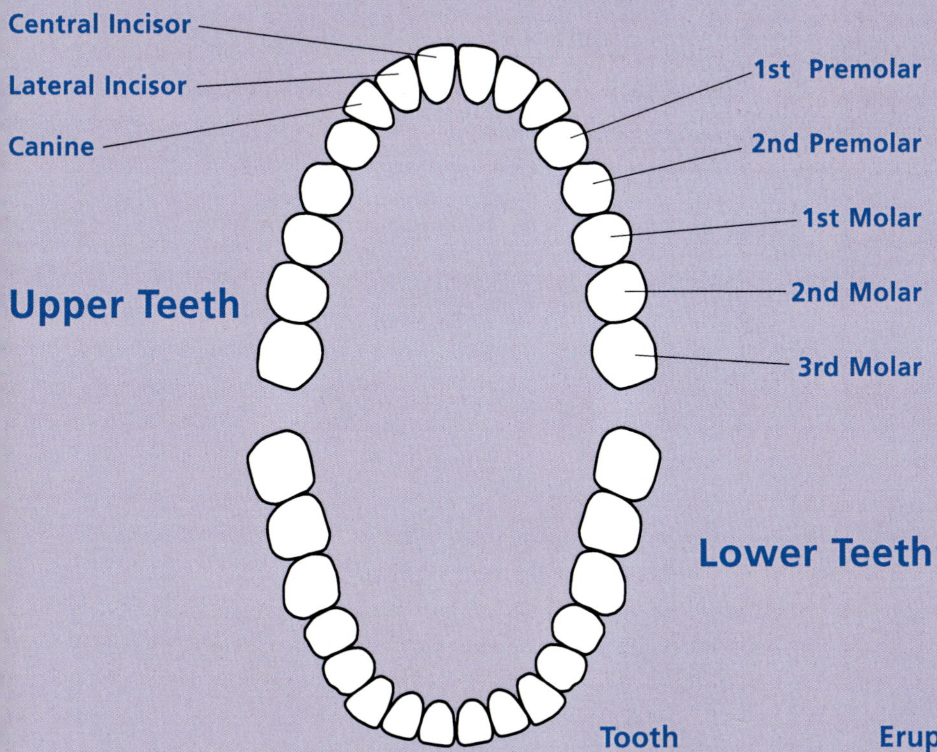

Tooth	Eruption Age
8 Incisors	7 - 9 years
2 Lower Canines	9 - 10 years
2 Upper Canines	12 - 13 years
4 First Premolars	10 - 11 years
4 Second Premolars	10 - 12 years
4 First Molars	6 - 7 years
4 Second Molars	12 - 13 years
4 Third Molars (wisdom teeth)	17 - 21 years

"I need parental supervision."

Did You Know?

"I'm now at the age when you need to pay special attention to my jaw and the bite relationship of my teeth."

"My dentist and hygienist say you should supervise my brushing and flossing until I'm 8 or 9."

"I have to floss...

- Gently place the floss between the teeth so that it rests just below the gumline.
- With a front-to-back motion and holding the floss tight against the tooth, bring the floss up the side of the tooth until it reaches the biting surface.

... and brush my WHOLE mouth!"

Remember, the goal is to remove ALL the plaque from *ALL* the surfaces of your child's teeth, gums, tongue and cheeks!

- Begin the process by holding the side of the soft bristles gently against the gum below the level of the tooth.
- Move the brush in small circular movements towards the tooth, along the gum line and to the biting surface of the tooth. This must be done gently and thoroughly.
- To brush the biting surface, use the tops of the bristles and scrub thoroughly, getting in all the grooves.
- Have your dentist instruct you on the method he or she suggests as best for your particular needs.

"Even when I'm bigger, I still need to be reminded of the correct way to brush and floss."

"My teeth need
a sporting chance."

"Custom mouthguards will protect my teeth, jaw, jaw bone joints and brain during sports."

Custom mouthguards get used because they feel more secure and comfortable compared to regular mouthguards.

What's more:

- They don't interfere with speech.
- They don't interfere with breathing.
- THEY PROTECT!

Custom mouthguards should be used for:

- gymnastics
- cycling
- ski racing
- weightlifting
- contact sports including baseball, football, basketball, rugby, soccer, field and ice hockey, lacrosse, volleyball.

Did You Know?

Sports and playground activities are a major source of serious dental injuries.

"Don't let my special needs stop me from getting regular dental care!"

Some children are born with a life-long physical or mental disability, while others may be diagnosed at any age with a medical condition which may last a lifetime.

Some children may require surgery, an organ transplant, drug therapy or radiation treatment due to a medical condition.

Still others may experience a significant injury or burn to the face or body in their young lives.

Whatever their situation, these children need regular dental care.

For children with special medical needs, prolonged dental neglect can cause serious, even life-threatening complications.

At the very least, dental neglect can lead to decay, gum disease, bad breath and tooth loss.

Restorative dental procedures may not be possible later because of the medical circumstances or physical disability involved.

For example, persons with seizure disorders, cerebral palsy, developmental delay or similar conditions are not able to wear any removable appliances such as dentures.

In other cases, the visible outcome of dental neglect can impede one's ability to integrate into employment and social circles.

Missing teeth, discolored, malformed or unevenly spaced teeth create social stigma and psychological burdens associated with these characteristics.

For more information, speak with your local Pediatric Dental Specialist. Or contact one of the following organizations:

American Academy of Pediatric Dentistry
Suite 700
211 E. Chicago Avenue,
Chicago, Illinois 60611
Tel. (312) 337-2169
Fax (312) 337-6329
Email: aapdinfo@aapd.org
Internet: www.aapd.org

Canadian Dental Association
1815 Alta Vista
Ottawa, Ontario K1G 3Y6
Tel. (613) 523-1770
Fax (613) 523-7736
Email: reception@cda-adc.ca
Internet: www.cda-adc.ca

Federation of Special Care Organizations in Dentistry
211 E. Chicago Avenue
Chicago, Illinois 60611
Tel. (312) 440-2500
Fax (312) 440-2800

“My teeth look great because I feed them well.”

"There are snacks which help keep my teeth HEALTHY...

- celery
- carrots and fresh vegetables
- cheese
- plain popcorn
- apples
- oranges
- plums
- peaches
- pears
- pineapple
- strawberries
- melon
- grapes
- grapefruit
- milk
- natural yogurt
- snack foods and beverages made with "xylitol", a natural sweetener that helps prevent cavities

and snacks to AVOID!"

- sticky foods and sugars
- chocolate bars
- candied apples
- candied popcorn
- toffees
- fruit roll-ups
- raisins and dried fruits
- suckers
- ju-jubes
- sweet licorice
- cookies and cakes
- sweetened carbonated beverages (including diet pops and iced tea drinks)

"Saliva keeps me smiling."

"The saliva in my mouth plays a number of significant roles, no matter how old I am."

- Neutralizes bacterial acid production.
- Acts as a reservoir for fluoride.
- Protects hard and soft tissues from drying out.
- Improves tastes.
- Lubricates the mouth to aid in chewing and swallowing.
- Prevents scratching of the soft tissues and the esophagus.
- Helps wash away food particles and dissolve sugars.
- Starts the digestion process.
- Under normal healthy conditions, saliva is filled with calcium and phosphate - the principal minerals that make up dental enamel.
- Some scientists think of saliva as a form of liquid enamel.
- Saliva bathes the teeth with its valuable minerals and helps heal initial decalcification lesions (the first stage of a cavity's formation).
- Salivary elements also discourage the growth of bacteria.

What exactly are plaque and decay?

- Plaque is a sticky compound made up primarily of salivary proteins, bacteria and particles of food.
- If allowed to mature over 24 hours, plaque promotes the production of acids.
- These acids demineralize (breakdown) the enamel, and so a cavity begins!
- The process is progressive. The bacteria moves inward to the next layer of the tooth - the dentin - and destroys it. We call this process decay.
- The main bacteria associated with the process of decay is ***streptococcus mutans***.
- "Xylitol", a natural sweetener and sugar substitute, effectively inhibits the development of cavity- causing streptococcus mutans bacteria.
- Unrestricted feeding habits and repeated exposure to sugars over extended periods of time during the day and at night influence the extent of decay.

Decayed Tooth

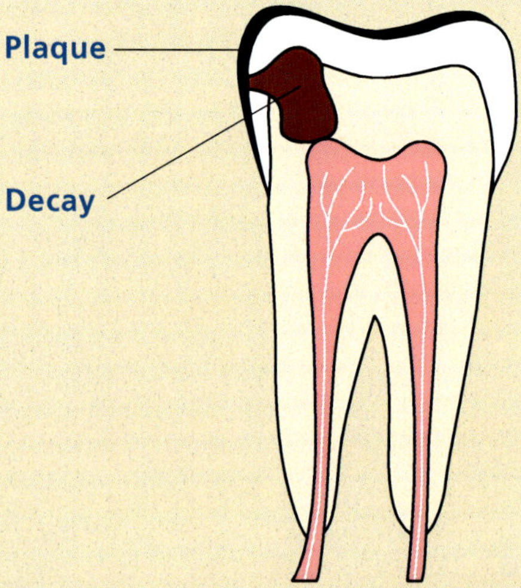

Healthy Tooth

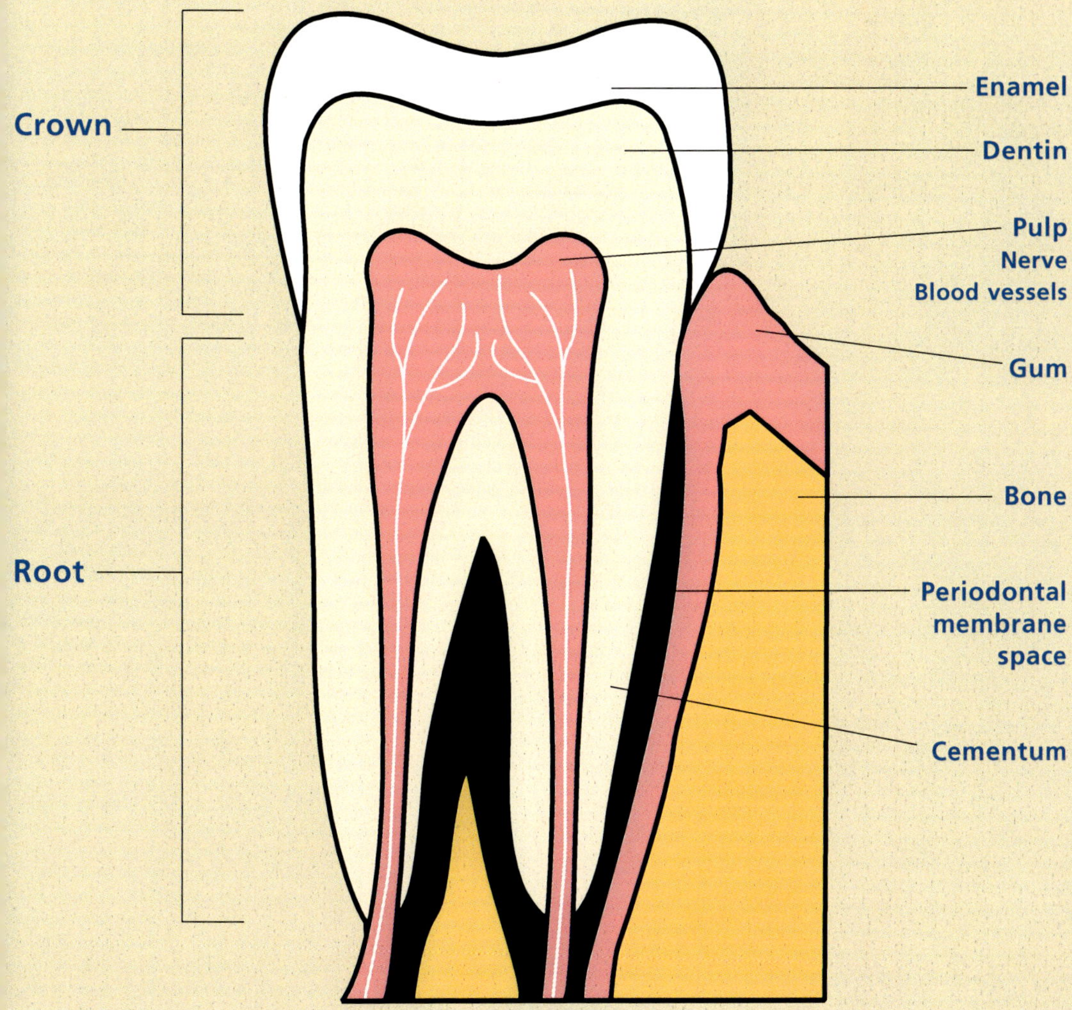

Permanent Teeth

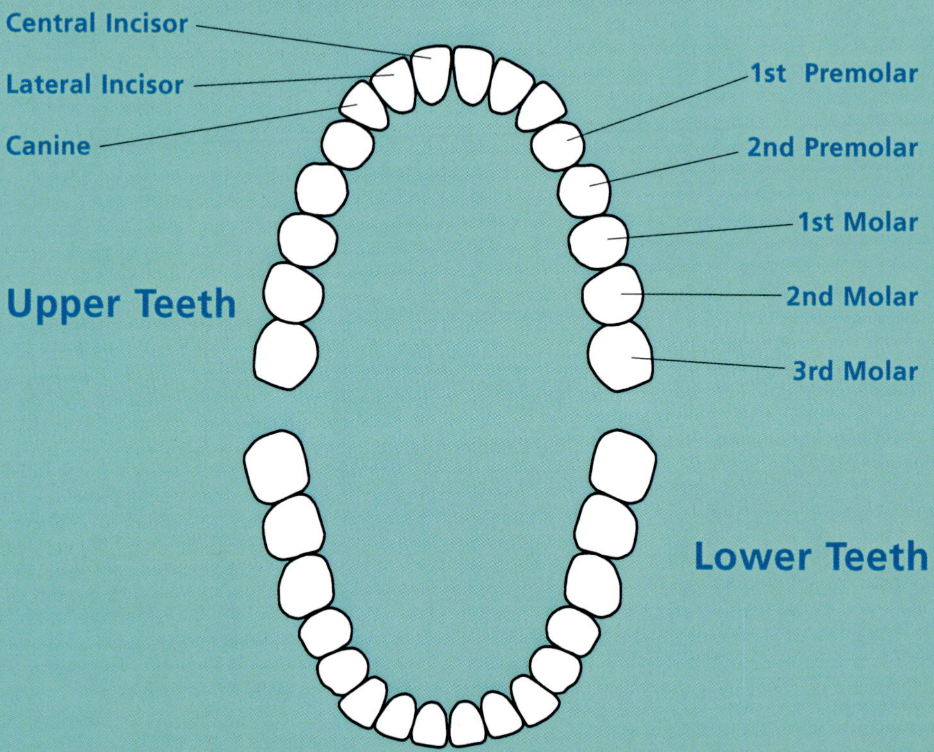

MY Name:

"Hey Mom and Dad! Use this page to record the dates when my permanent teeth first appear."

Upper Teeth:

	Left	Right
Central Incisor	____________	____________
Lateral Incisor	____________	____________
Canine	____________	____________
1st Premolar	____________	____________
2nd Premolar	____________	____________
1st Molar	____________	____________
2nd Molar	____________	____________
3rd Molar	____________	____________

Lower Teeth:

	Left	Right
Central Incisor	____________	____________
Lateral Incisor	____________	____________
Canine	____________	____________
1st Premolar	____________	____________
2nd Premolar	____________	____________
1st Molar	____________	____________
2nd Molar	____________	____________
3rd Molar	____________	____________

MY Notes